Do your laundry or you'll die alone

Advice your mom would give if she thought you were listening

Becky Blades

sourcebooks

Published by Sourcebooks, Inc.
P.O. Box 4410, Naperville, Illinois 60567-4410
(630) 961-3900
Fax: (630) 961-2168
www.sourcebooks.com

Originally published in 2014 in the United States by Startistry Publishing.

Printed and bound in China.

QL 10 9 8 7 6 5 4

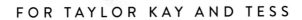

FOR TAYLOR KAY AND TESS

INTRODUCTION

Coming-of-age can be a messy, risky business.

Getting a job, keeping a friend, and finding love can each feel like life or death endeavors. And they can hinge on the tiniest things—often on things your mother told you when you were pretending to listen. Remember that time?

As a young woman today, you have skills that seem like superpowers. You can conduct a text argument with your two best friends without breaking parental eye contact. With a simple Google search, you can find answers to most of the practical questions that your mom's generation had to phone home for.

But what you *cannot* find on the Internet is your mother's voice—the voice that loves you, the voice that wants the best for you, and the voice that can autorepeat inside your head with tidbits of wisdom to keep you safe, centered, and slightly annoyed.

Because maybe, just maybe, she's right.

FOREWORD

A year before she graduated high school, when it hit me that my first-born daughter would soon be leaving home for college, I became overwhelmed by a frantic urgency. She wasn't ready.

She had worked hard to earn grades and SAT scores that put her in the running for the most selective colleges. She spoke French fluently. She knew how to handle a basketball and wield a microphone. And she knew how to parallel park. (Finally.) But NOT knowing what she DID NOT know was keeping me up at night.

In one of my Hollywood-lit nightmares, I saw her standing in the middle of a busy street, cars speeding toward her, her high-heel caught in a grate, trying desperately to save the shoe. Did I forget that lesson? "Leave the shoe, honey! Save yourself!"

So many things that seem like common sense have come to us through our mothers' words sprinkled and repeated through the years. As I prepared to let my daughter go, I could not help but wonder if my teachings had made it through the noise of the past eighteen years. Did she hear the rules of thumb and the cautionary tales? Were they even relevant? Did she know what she needed to know to take care of herself in this digitized, supersized world?

Even though she still had a few months left at home, I knew it was too late to fill the gaps in my parenting. My daughter had stopped listening.

So, did I let her go with my blessing, trusting that she would get her lessons as she needed them?

Not on your life.

I bit my tongue and quietly collected the advice that I thought she should have. When she left for college, I put it all in a good-bye letter and threatened to publish it on her Facebook page.

Dear Taylor,

Though you may think I've driven you half-crazy with reminders and lessons this past year, I've kept a lot of things to myself. Hush. I have.

Here are a few things that college will not teach you. Some are things I've told you a hundred times. Some are things that have never come up. Mostly, they are things that would make you roll your eyes if I said them in person.

So indulge me. I know you don't need another lecture, honey. But I need to give you one. (There. Right there. I saw that eye roll!)

Love Always,
Mom

DO YOUR LAUNDRY OR YOU'LL DIE ALONE.

Yes, we're starting here.

Do your laundry regularly. Try every week. Do it before you run out of clean underwear and before you need your favorite jeans. Because when you want your favorite jeans, and only your favorite jeans will do, you will want them clean. You will not want to be in the dilemma of choosing between dirty, stinky favorite jeans and jeans that make your butt look (choose one: wide, low, flat, etc.).

Either of these less-than-perfect options will undermine your self-confidence, and you will not have the courage to talk to that cute guy. And then you may never get another chance and…then comes the dying alone part.

02

IF YOU CAN'T SAY SOMETHING NICE, DON'T SAY ANYTHING AT ALL.

You're smart enough to think of something nice.

03

SPEAK CLEARLY.

Enunciate. Articulate. Spit out your gum.

04

WHEN SOMEONE ASKS FOR HELP, ALWAYS GIVE HER SOMETHING.

You don't have to give her what she asks for, but you can give her a word of encouragement, a helpful idea, or a caring glance.

05

KEEP YOUR COLORS SEPARATE—BUT ONLY IN THE LAUNDRY.

If you wash a red T-shirt with a white T-shirt, you will get a faded red T-shirt and a nasty pink T-shirt. If you wash a black T-shirt with a white T-shirt, you will get a linty black T-shirt and a splotchy purply grey T-shirt.

When you paint a picture, and you absolutely should every now and then, you almost never get what you want straight from the tube. You must mix colors on your palette to get what you need. This can be a metaphor for whatever you like.

06

KEEP AT LEAST ONE STUFFED ANIMAL.

07

LIVE. *And let live.*

Live well, my dear. Live large. Live out loud. Live with each cell. Live each challenge, as if it is a way to prove that you are alive. Live each moment, as if there are no do-overs. And then, if you want to, do them over. Some days, it will seem like God gave you so much energy and ability, that one mere body cannot do them justice in a 24-hour day. Some days, it will take all you have just to sit in a chair and exist. Some days, sitting in a chair will be all you need to feel true joy.

And some days, the fullness of your own life will not be enough. And you will want to control how someone else lives hers. Don't.

08

That said, FRIENDS DON'T LET FRIENDS:
- drive drunk
- text while driving
- get discount body art

09

A FRIEND WHO IS MAD AT YOU FOR TAKING HER CAR KEYS IS BETTER THAN A DEAD FRIEND.

10

THE NUMBER ONE CAUSE OF GUILT IS DOING SOMETHING WRONG.

11

DON'T LOSE your HEAD in your STUFF.

Possessions can be fulfilling to acquire, and they can make our lives easier or more fun. But keep *things* in perspective. Holding on to too much stuff keeps our hands full and our heads in a bad place.

12

USE LESS SALT AND MORE PEPPER.

13

THERE'S NOTHING WORSE THAN A SMART GIRL WHO ACTS DUMB.

14

MONEY IS THE EASIEST THING TO REPLACE.

You can always make more money. Time, relationships, dignity, trust, and reputation, on the other hand, are hard to come by. They are hard to create the first time and virtually impossible to replace. Don't sell them short; don't sell them out for one another; and whatever you do, don't sell them for mere money.

15

WASH OFF YOUR MAKEUP
BEFORE YOU GO TO BED.

16

KNOW GOD.

17

Just because someone is the love of your life doesn't mean that
he will automatically know what you want for your birthday.

SPEAK UP.

18

MAKE SOMETHING EVERY DAY.

Make a meal or a joke or a scarf or a poem. Make a notecard or a paper doll or a dress for yourself. Make a face or a friend or a Facebook friend. Creating is your birthright, and celebrating your creativity reminds you of your unique place in the world.

19

NEVER PUT ANYTHING ON THE INTERNET THAT YOU WOULD NOT WANT TO DISCUSS:

- in a job interview
- on a first date
- with your mother

20

ALWAYS OWN A BIKE.

21

NEVER LIE TO YOUR MOTHER.
And if you do, never think you got away with it.

22

CUT PEOPLE SOME SLACK.

If we live life full-out, we will be wronged and disappointed many times over—not because people are mean or because we deserve it, but because life, for all of us, is on-the-job training. Most people in our lives are doing the best they can with the training they have; so sometimes what seems like negligence or cruelty is simply someone trying to navigate a moment that she was not prepared for.

23

PUT THE LID BACK ON THE MILK.

24

DON'T HEAT-DRY YOUR DELICATES.

25

POLITICS AND RELIGION WILL ALWAYS BE DELICATE SUBJECTS.

Give them the care they deserve, and don't let things heat up.

26

DON'T PRESS 'SEND' IN THE HEAT OF EMOTION.

Your frustration with someone will go away with time, but those characters in cyberspace can exist forever.

27

USE IT OR LOSE IT.

This goes for skills, brain cells, muscles, friendships, foreign languages, and native tongues. It may also go for freedoms, property, and cherished beliefs.

Employ and exercise the things you want to keep, or plan to spend extra time recovering them the next time you need them.

28

FAKE IT 'TIL YOU MAKE IT.

29

EVERYONE FEELS LIKE A FAKE.
Except the real fakes.

30

ADMIT

when you're wrong.

31

ADMIT

when you don't know something.

32

ADMIT

when you need to move up a size.

33

Don't trust the size on the clothing tag.

Always try on before you buy.

34

YOU ARE THE VIEW.

As you roll out of bed and into your sweats for an unstructured day, think about all the people who will be treated to the vision of you.

Most people care about what they are seeing, what they are hearing, and what they are smelling. Senses define the pleasure of our days. While skipping a shower or a shave might make your morning easier, it is not a victimless crime.

35

GOOD POSTURE IS SLIMMING.

36

A BAD ATTITUDE MAKES YOUR BUTT LOOK BIG.

37

READING IS SEXY.

38

YOUR CLOTHES SHOULD FIT.
Find a good tailor.

Your pants shouldn't drag on the ground. Your blouse should close in the front without the buttons screaming from the strain. The shoulders of your jacket should sit on the shoulders of your body without wandering off. A nip here and a tuck there doesn't cost that much; they can make a world of difference in the impression you make.

39

TAKE NOTES IN CLASS,

even if you don't need them. They will remind you of what is important to the teacher.

40

TAKE NOTES OUTSIDE OF CLASS.

These luscious years will be rich with love and learning. Keep a journal. Record your joys, your heartbreaks, and your epiphanies. *You'll treasure it beyond measure.*

41

IT'S EASIER TO HIT ALL THE NOTES IF YOU KNOW YOUR RANGE.

42

WHEN SINGING the American national anthem, pick your key with the high note in mind. Or, if you're singing with the crowd at a ball game, just lip-synch the high notes like everybody else.

43

HAVE AT LEAST ONE FRIEND WITH A GUITAR.

44

PLANT A TREE.

If you plant a seedling today, in twenty years, you will see a landscape transformed. Nothing feels quite like it.

45

GIVE MONEY OR HELP to whomever you think

needs it. Don't spend too much time agonizing over whether your gift to the begging woman on the corner will be spent on a bottle for a baby or a bottle for her. The decision to give is a decision between you and God. What she does with it is between her and God.

46

HOWEVER, if you know someone spent her last $20 on

crack cocaine or a bottle of gin, don't give her your last $20.

Don't worry, you'll know.

<u>CHARITY</u> begins at home.

You'll be in a better position to save the homeless if you know how you're going to pay your rent this month.

PETITES SORTIES

Dans ce numéro :
UN ROMAN COMPLET

BE the HOSTESS.

Want to make others feel at ease and make yourself feel more confident? Assume the role of hostess. No matter where you are, act welcoming and caring, and you will come off like you own the place: "Hello, I'm so glad to see you, did you have any trouble getting here?" or "I was just headed to the food table, are you hungry?" or "This is my planet, can I help you find your way around?"

49

ALWAYS SEND BACK THE RSVP.

If someone takes the time to invite you, you can take the time to reply. Not to is rude.

Mothers often catch the blame for lapses in etiquette. Please show people your mama raised you right.

50

DON'T WAIT to be invited to the movies, dinner, or a night on the town. Sometimes—at least half the time—you should do the inviting. A lot of the time, you should be the party planner.

51

When you propose a toast to someone, look at them. Remember that it's about them, not you.

52

LISTEN MORE AND TALK LESS.

53

ASK QUALITY QUESTIONS.

You'll be more desirable company when you show your interest with the right type of questions.

Open-ended questions allow people to take the conversation where they want to. Example: "How was your week?"

Specific questions let people know you have been listening. Example: "What did you wind up doing with that stray ferret you brought home last week?"

54

KEEP YOUR HANDS
BELOW YOUR SHOULDERS.

That's the easiest way to assure you won't: pick your teeth, touch your face, twirl your hair, wipe your nose, rub your eyes, smear your makeup, and any number of other unattractive nervous habits.

55

HAVE AT LEAST ONE OUTFIT
THAT MAKES YOU FEEL LIKE
A MILLION BUCKS.

Wear it until your friends start complaining.

56

DO SOMETHING NICE OR GOOD EVERY DAY AND TELL NO ONE.

Be kind to an animal, give an atta-girl to a YouTube posting, give money to a good cause, or pick up some litter in the park.

Sweet secrets are winks between you and God, and they remind you of your pure goodness and strength.

57

GIVE SOME THOUGHT TO HOW YOU WILL PLAY IT WHEN ROBOTS TAKE OVER THE WORLD.

When the time comes, you may not have time to ponder your decisions.

58

EVEN SLOPPY PEOPLE PREFER NEAT ROOMMATES.

Sad, but true. Pick up your stuff.

59

TEST THE HEAT OF YOUR IRON ON A HIDDEN SEAM OR HEM.

Iron-shaped holes on the front of your dress can ruin the look you're going for. *Or, if you must, get a steamer.*

60

DON'T WAD UP YOUR CLOTHES.

Some morning, today's dirty shirt or sweater will be your cleanest option, and you'll want to tell yourself that you can wear it and no one will be the wiser. You might get away with it, if it has not been squashed under a wet towel for two days.

61

HANGERS HELP.

Folding things on a shelf or in a drawer is a good way to keep them off the floor. But smashing and stacking folded clothes can create fold wrinkles that are only slightly better than floor wrinkles. Hangers to the rescue! Use nonslip hangers for slippery blouses and clip hangers for skirts and pants. Drape everything else—from flowing blouses to silk scarves—over a pants hanger.

62

LINT IS NEVER IN STYLE.

Get a lint brush, or make one out of tape.

THANK-YOU notes are **ALWAYS** in style.

It will always be difficult to know what to do and say when someone disappoints or hurts you. But when someone makes a good difference in your life, the one right thing to do is to make absolutely sure that she knows it. Say "thank you."

Say it like you mean it—with sincerity, details, and reasons that will convince your recipient that she is Nobel-worthy and that you did not merely recycle the note thanking Aunt Ruth for your birthday cookie bouquet.

Every once in a while, write a thank-you note as if you're competing for a prize. Compose it with care and purpose and literary flourish, as if your future depends on it. Make it something that the recipient will want to keep on the nightstand or tucked away like a treasure to cheer her when she thinks her life has not mattered.

64

HOLD BABIES WHENEVER YOU GET A CHANCE. It's good for both of you.

65

IT'S OKAY TO FAVOR FAMILY.

It's true in all cultures. Family members merit priority placement and special treatment. Everyone will understand why you choose your sister as your maid of honor, your dad as your first dance, and your mother as your plus-one at that first Oscar party. (I am pretty sure that this is Hollywood protocol.)

66

NEPOTISM IS NOT AS EASY AS IT SOUNDS.

Yes, everyone expects you to pick your sister as your maid of honor; but if you cast her in a play or hire her for a job, she will have to be twice as good or work twice as hard as everyone else.

IF YOU HAVE A BOOK IN YOU, FOR GOODNESS' SAKE, LET IT OUT.

Creative humans walk around with all kinds of things stuck inside: songs, screenplays, passionate love poems, and wild works of art. Maybe that's why people seem so tense: a simple case of overcrowding. Learn the joy of letting your expressions and creations out into the world. Don't do it for money or fame, but simply to get the beauty out where it can be found by others.

You will breathe more deeply, what with all the extra room inside.

68

MAYBE, IT'S NOT A BOOK AFTER ALL.

Not every idea or life experience is enough for a book. Maybe it's a short story or a blog article. Perhaps it's a T-shirt slogan. Or maybe, it's just something you should keep in your journal.

69

MEMORIZE A PASSAGE OF YOUR FAVORITE BOOK OR STORY.

When you commit something to memory, it becomes a part of you. It is a treasure that no one can take and a treat that you can call out at whim to entertain or comfort you, no batteries or Wi-Fi required.

70

STRETCH.

DON'T PUT OFF STARTING SOMETHING BECAUSE YOU AREN'T SURE YOU CAN FINISH IT.

If you get the urge to begin something—an article, a social movement, a letter to your mom—go ahead and start it. The creative energy is strongest at the inception of the idea; and when you get momentum going, you might just find the time and resources to take it all the way. Only one thing is *sure* to keep you from finishing:

NOT STARTING.

72

GET ENOUGH SLEEP.

73

GET A CUTE UMBRELLA.

74

IF YOU WANT TO SHORTEN AN ARGUMENT, BREAK INTO A FRENCH ACCENT.

Or a bad British accent. Or any accent, for that matter.

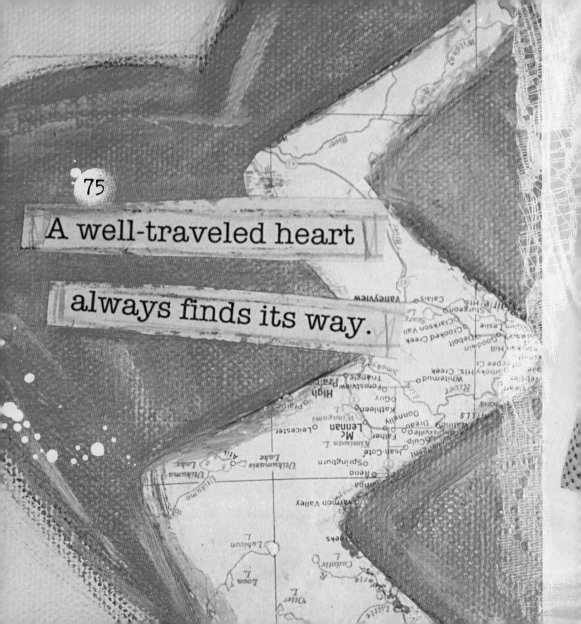

75

A well-traveled heart

always finds its way.

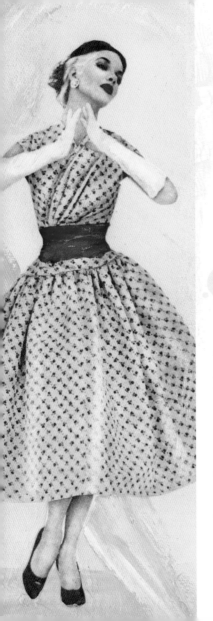

76

PLAN a TRIP to PARIS.

Though it may be a faraway fantasy, setting your sights on a trip to Paris releases your inner French girl and makes every day more chic.

Studying Paris—or any place you long to visit—is a luscious way to spend your web-surfing time. By the time you get there, it will feel like a long-lost friend.

77

WHEREVER YOU ARE, BE ALL THERE.

78

YOUR THOUGHTS ARE YOUR THINGS.

You can decide what to think about and which thoughts to keep company
with. If you know you are hosting a toxic, judgmental thought, it is
your responsibility to talk to the thought and set it straight, or to send it
packing. Who else is going to do it?

79

RAINBOWS ARE PRETTIER WHEN YOU'RE WEARING YELLOW SHOES.

No one knows why.

80

DON'T GIVE IN TO BULLIES.

81

WHEN SOMETHING IS BOTHERING YOU, TAKE IT FOR A WALK.

There is something about walking that clears the mind and brightens the outlook. Maybe it is the endorphins or the dopamine or getting oxygen to the brain…or maybe it is the step-by-step reminder that simply by putting one foot in front of the other, we can make the scenery change.

82

DON'T BE AFRAID TO WEAR A HAT.
Just know what kind you look good in.

83

OWN A TUTU AND A BOA.
Because you just never know.

84

BUILD A GOOD REPUTATION.
IT'S SIMPLE, BUT NOT EASY:
- Be nice to people.
- Do what you say you will do.

85

LITTLE HABITS CAN COST YOU BIG.

Let's say, just hypothetically, that you are in the grips of an expensive beverage addiction. You line up, day after day, to pay for a pricey coffee, rather than serving yourself for pennies at home.

The $4 a day you spend on fancy coffee adds up to $1,460 a year, which would be enough to put you in a decent used car. But you won't buy it. The car, that is. Because you bought the coffee.

So, think hard before you start smoking or hoarding cats.

86

HANDLE DISAPPOINTMENT

in private, if possible, and always with grace.

87

WHEN YOU'RE HAPPY,
TELL YOUR FACE ABOUT IT.

When you're not, don't let your face be your tell.

88

WHEN YOU MAKE A CAKE FOR SOMEONE, MAKE A CUPCAKE OUT OF THE BATTER FOR YOURSELF.

Only so you can be sure you didn't use salt instead of sugar. That's the only reason.

EXPECTATIONS ARE POWERFUL THINGS.

Learn to control them.

LEARN TO APOLOGIZE.

Relationships don't come with erasers, but you have something close: apologies. Few things honor and heal a relationship like a genuine, "I'm sorry."

Make sure you mean it. A true apology expresses responsibility, regret, and an interest in making things better. With practice, you will learn how to erase hurt and bad feelings quickly, and how to go back for a second pass, if you need to—without rubbing an ugly hole in the page.

91

BLACK is the NEW BLACK.

Black is not back because black was never gone.

92

DON'T JOG IN A PARK AFTER DARK.

93

BUT DO JOG IN THE PARK.

94

MAKE NEW FRIENDS
AND KEEP THE OLD.

New friends pull you forward; old friends keep you grounded.
It's a healthy stretching exercise.

95

Profanity doesn't make you sound more dramatic or serious.

IT JUST MAKES YOU SOUND
#!%*ING PROFANE.

96

When your best friend's boyfriend breaks up with her,

RESIST THE URGE TO COMFORT
HER BY CURSING HIM.
They will probably get back together tomorrow.

97

PAYING RETAIL IS A SIGN OF WEAKNESS.
Except for gifts, such as books. Like this one, for example.

98

HAVE A LIST OF THINGS YOU LIKE TO DO THAT DON'T COST MONEY.

99

BAKING SODA IS CHEAP
and does 52 amazing things.

100

PAY YOURSELF FIRST.

As soon as you start earning money, you will start paying people some of it: the landlord, the tax man, and the woman who does your pedicures.

One day, you'll add it up and realize that you've earned hundreds of thousands of dollars, and all you have to show for it is a spotty credit score. As you gaze upon your interest-accruing credit card statement asking, "So this is the minimum payment?," the savings-savvy lady who polished your toenails may be leaning over her cruise ship balcony rail asking, "So this is Martinique?"

Put 10 percent of what you earn in a savings account to accumulate your own wealth and security. You won't miss it, if you get in the habit early. Pay yourself first, and no matter whom else you pay, you're moving forward with your goals. (When times get tight, you might need to do your own pedicures.)

101

DON'T use the phone while you're driving. If you don't trust yourself not to talk or text, put your phone on silent in the backseat.

102

DON'T APPLY MAKEUP while you're driving. The driver behind you can't see your face, but you're ruining his mood.

103

DON'T THINK YOU'RE INVISIBLE while you're driving, especially at stoplights. Cameras are everywhere.

104

IF YOU DAMAGE SOMEONE'S CAR IN THE PARKING LOT, leave a sincere "I'm sorry" note with your insurance agent's phone number. Then call your agent, so she can expect the call. Don't leave your name or any other personal information.

105

HAVE EXTRA SETS OF KEYS MADE, and give one set to a neighbor you trust.

106

IF YOU DON'T KNOW WHERE ALL YOUR KEYS ARE, HAVE YOUR LOCKS CHANGED.

107

PARK IN THE SHADE in the
summer and in the sunshine in the winter.

108

LEARN HOW TO DRIVE A STICK SHIFT.
Your world adventures may take you to places without automatic transmissions.

109

CHOOSE YOUR BATTLES.
The fewer the better. Life is not war.

110

WHEN YOU GET SOMETHING NEW,
DECIDE WHERE YOU WILL KEEP IT
AND PUT IT THERE.

111

PUT VALUABLES IN A SAFE PLACE—
but not so safe that you cannot find them later.

112

ONLY ONE JUNK DRAWER PER ROOM.

A well-tamed junk drawer is okay, but be careful. Don't feed those hungry catch-all places, where old phone chargers commingle with almost-read mail and cottage cheese lids. These are evil quicksands of confusion and despair. If you give them any nourishment at all, they will grow with abandon, consuming your peace of mind, your valuable countertop space, and uncashed checks from home.

113

RECYCLE.

Plastic bags can now be recycled into rain boots.

114

REUSE.

Your mother's old rain boots are perfectly functional.

115

REPURPOSE.

Your childhood rain boots make great flower pots.

116

RECONSIDER.
Decide. Move forward.

But when things don't go to plan or you get new information, think again. In today's fast-changing world and your fast-changing stage of life, yesterday's sure bet is today's long shot. Looking critically at decisions you have made is not weak or wishy-washy, it's just plain smart.

117

LATHER. RINSE. *Repeating is optional.*

118

KEEP YOUR HOUSEHOLD CLEANING
PRODUCTS SEPARATE FROM YOUR
PERSONAL HYGIENE PRODUCTS.
Using Pledge instead of hairspray can set back your morning.

119

REPLACE THE TOILET PAPER ROLL
WHEN YOU USE THE LAST OF IT.
Every time. Always. Even if it's in the closet across the hall. Or in
the downstairs pantry. Or in the basement.

120

DON'T TELL BATHROOM JOKES AT THE KITCHEN TABLE.

121

DON'T TELL INSIDE JOKES AROUND OUTSIDE COMPANY.

Nobody likes to feel left out. Having a laugh that does not include everyone is rude and hurtful to people who don't know you well. If you are the hostess, it is unforgivable.

By the way, laughing at that thing on your phone that no one can see counts, too.

122

BE the kind of NEIGHBOR you WANT to HAVE.

MULTITASKING DOESN'T ALWAYS SAVE YOU TIME.

Doing two things at once makes a girl feel like she's taming her calendar. But efficient as it may seem, dividing your attention between high-focus tasks causes mistakes and slows you down. Some things deserve full focus.

That said, some things can be juggled: you can always call your mom while you're waiting for a load in the dryer.

124

CHEW WITH YOUR MOUTH CLOSED.

125

FIND A DENTIST
YOU ARE NOT AFRAID OF.

126

FLOSS.

127

A BARK IS NOT WORSE THAN A BITE.

When dogs get frightened, they bark and bite. Men can behave like dogs when they get frightened. So don't give up on a perfectly good man just for barking. Biting, however, is never okay.

128

THINGS BREAK.

One of the hardest parts of growing up is realizing that nearly everything breaks or wears out.

Don't let it derail you. Fix what you can and accept what you can't. And save the broken pieces, just in case.

129

GET A TOOLBOX, A SEWING KIT, AND A CAN-DO ATTITUDE.

Now, you can fix anything, except a bad neighbor or a broken heart.

130

SOME RULES ARE MADE TO BE BROKEN.

Laws are not.

131

POP-TARTS ARE THE BEST QUICK-FIX BREAK UP FOOD.

I can't remember if I read this in a *USA Today* survey or on Wikipedia, but it is a proven fact. In limited quantities, Pop-Tarts have healing powers. They can be purchased over the counter in convenience stores at all hours, and you can keep them in your car. If a toaster is unavailable, I recommend dipping them in ice cream and eating them in your sweatpants.

132

MAKE SURE YOUR FRIENDS KNOW YOUR FAVORITE ICE-CREAM FLAVOR.

133

FIND a HEALTHY FOOD you LIKE

that does not need refrigeration.
Nuts, fruit, a light protein bar; keep some in
your purse or car at all times. It will save you
from hitting the vending machine in a weak
moment.

134

EAT YOUR VEGETABLES.

135

BE A VEGAN, IF YOU WANT TO.
But don't make everyone else suffer for it.

136

LEAVE YOUR CAMPGROUND BETTER THAN YOU FOUND IT.

In the urban world, this means cleaning your table at Starbucks, moving the shopping cart out of the middle of the parking lot, and letting the store clerk know when the restroom is out of toilet paper.

137

LOOK PEOPLE IN THE EYE.
You'll discover that this is hard to do while looking at your phone.

138

LISTEN.
No, but really. Listen.

139

IF PEOPLE CAN'T TELL YOU'RE LISTENING, YOU'RE PROBABLY NOT.

140

POCKET YOUR CELL PHONE DURING MEALS.

If you're eating alone, it's your call. But if you are dining with others, your call is a slap in their face. Even looking at your phone is rude. Turn it off. Don't answer if it rings. Put it away.

141

PUT YOUR NAPKIN ON YOUR LAP.

And don't blow your nose with it. And don't hide your phone there. *No one is falling for it.*

142

ALWAYS CARRY SOME CASH.

143

CHECK YOUR POCKETS.

Before you do your own laundry or hand clothes over to the dry cleaner, check every single pocket. This means putting your hand all the way into the pockets, not just scrunching the pants in search of foreign shapes. Paper, which can be of great value, is quite soft, especially after it's been marinating in the bottom of a dirty clothes hamper. A pen in the laundry can ruin a whole load; and washing a love note or meeting reminder can ruin your whole week.

Your mother may not have mentioned this, likely because the things you left in your pockets over the years would have broken your heart or embarrassed you both. And if she found money in your pockets, she likely considered it God's little thank-you tips.

A MOTHER IS ONLY AS HAPPY AS HER SADDEST CHILD. SO TELL YOUR MOM WHEN THE CRISIS IS OVER.

Text your mom when the test you told her you were dreading turns out fine. Call her when the boss who was picking on you commends your work.

And when the guy who broke up with you this morning calls to make up tonight, don't wait until NEXT WEEK to tell your mom the tragedy is over. Leave out the make-up details, but tell your mom you're happy again. She worries.

145

USE TITLES OF RESPECT.

Call your friend's dad "Mr.," even if he says you don't have to. If you know someone is a doctor, call her "Dr." She worked hard for it.

146

OFFER YOUR SEAT to anyone older or less healthy than you. And occasionally to someone who made an inappropriate shoe choice.

147

EVERYONE DESERVES A RESPONSE.

Return phone calls and emails.

A TOUS PROPR bainset
signature 5¼ p. p.
caire DUPIN, 38, ru

GRATUITEMENT

LE CRIME DE VIESLY

Malgré ses dénégations Paul Deudon
a été inculpé d'assassinat et écroué

LILLE, 20 septembre. — Télégr. Matin.
— L'interrogatoire

Cartes Postales
ANTIGE, Aubenas (A

TARIFAGES

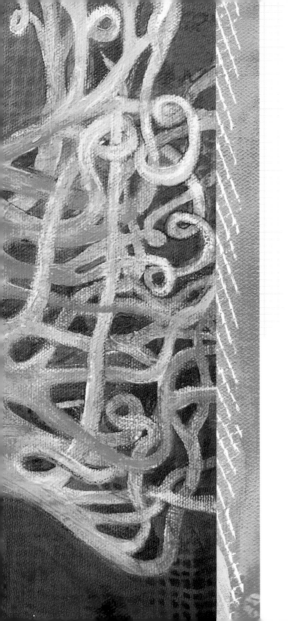

148

Let your ROOTS run away from home.

You can put down roots anywhere that you decide, but you never have to feel stuck. It's a great big world out there, so try some cities and neighborhoods on for size. It's easier when you're young.

149

THE QUALITY OF YOUR FRIENDS CAN DEFINE THE QUALITY OF YOUR LIFE.

150

FORGIVE QUICKLY.

Time lost holding grudges is time truly lost. But that's not the worst part. Storing or feeding a grievance too long makes it feel at home. Once it unpacks, a grievance morphs into resentment, grows extra arms, eats all your favorite cereal, and never cuts its fingernails. Before you know it, you're housing a forgiveness-resistant gobble monster that is almost impossible to throw out.

151

VOTE.

152

VOLUNTEER.

153

READ THE INSTRUCTIONS.

154

DON'T CORRECT ANOTHER PERSON'S GRAMMAR, unless she asks you to or you're getting paid to do it.

155

KNOW

who your friends are.

156

KNOW

who your friends aren't.

157

KNOW

the difference between collecting and hoarding.

158

KNOW WHEN TO READ THE FINE PRINT.

When accepting *terms and conditions* of the wireless network at the airport, don't sweat the tiny type. But if you're signing a lease, an employment contract, or anything that makes you nervous, read it all. Then get a second set of eyes, just to be sure. Learning too late of a "double-rent-for-pets clause" can make that dream apartment a very stinky deal.

159

DON'T THINK YOU KNOW HOW IT FEELS

to be another race or gender, or to be older than you are. You cannot fathom the wisdom another person's experience gives him. As hard as you try to walk in another's shoes, true empathy means understanding that you may never really understand. *But keep trying.*

160

MOVE YOUR BODY.

Exercise makes everything better.

161

STILL YOUR MIND.

Meditation makes everything better.

162

FASTEN YOUR SEAT BELT.

Being alive makes everything better.

163

Absence **DOESN'T** make the heart grow fonder.

Maybe for a little while, absence helps you forget the irritating annoyances of a person. Loneliness might allow you to romanticize the way things were or might be again. And a little absence can be a nice break, which we all need—even from wonderful things like chocolate, coffee, and sisters.

But don't be fooled into thinking that being apart brings people closer together. Being apart keeps people apart.

164

KEEP

your knees together when you're sitting on stage.

165

KEEP

your head when all around you are losing theirs.

166

KEEP

your receipts.

167

BACK UP YOUR MEMORIES.

Though your mother's generation did not grow up with computers, she sees how much you entrust to those breakable, losable gadgets. And we have a different understanding of what's at stake with these new-age keepsake keepers.

You may have felt the agony of losing a term paper or an email thread. Well, my dear, that is nothing compared to the heartache you will feel at age 40, when you can't show your daughter the college application essay you're so proud of or the photos that will prove you could once do the splits.

Have a trustworthy backup system for your cyber keepsakes.

168

ALWAYS CARRY A NOTEPAD…
and maybe some colored pencils.

169

CHECK YOUR MATH.

170

HIDE YOUR CHOCOLATE.

You may need to hide it from your roommate, or you may need to hide it from yourself. The point is, some things are just too tempting to be left out in the open.

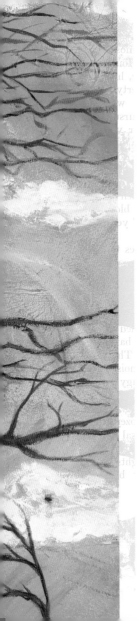

171

HANG AROUND at <u>HOME.</u>

Schedule a half-day each week at home, all to yourself…to turn off the phone and computer, to drift into your closet and put outfits together, to give yourself a facial, to look at your calendar and see what's coming up, to write a note to a friend, to think about what you need from the store, or to call your mom.

Avoid anything with a deadline, a grade, or a bill associated with it. Just be you in your space.

It feels indulgent, but it actually boosts productivity and reduces the stress of your week. But you must schedule it, or it may never happen.

172

BUY THE GENERIC BRAND WHEN IT DOESN'T MAKE A DIFFERENCE.

Medicines, paper products, salt, and pepper may cost less if you buy generic. Name brands can be 40 to 300 percent higher. But when you buy condoms, cold cuts, or chocolate, pay top dollar and heed the "sell by" date.

173

COOKED FOOD LASTS 3-4 DAYS IN THE REFRIGERATOR.

That's all. After that, you will have to throw it out.
Your mother will not be doing this anymore.

174

HAVE RUBBER GLOVES. On hand.

175

TO STERILIZE SOMETHING, YOU MUST LEAVE IT AT LEAST 15 MINUTES AT 121°C (250°F) OR 3 MINUTES AT 134°C (273°F). *Yes, you will need to know this.*

176

BIRTH CONTROL FAILS MORE THAN ONE PERCENT OF THE TIME.

177

DON'T ASSUME SOMEONE IS PREGNANT BY THE WAY SHE LOOKS.

There's no graceful way to take back, "When are you due?"

178

WHEN SOMEONE ASKS IF YOU ARE
AN ARTIST, ALWAYS SAY, "YES."

179

YOU CAN PUT OIL-BASED PAINT OVER
ACRYLIC PAINT, but not the other way around.

180

HAVE A FAVORITE POEM.

181

BE AN ORIGINAL.

Just be yourself, and you'll be a one and only. What's more, you'll be easy to authenticate.

182

NO ONE WILL MIND IF YOU STAND OUT, IF YOU DON'T TAKE YOURSELF TOO SERIOUSLY.

No one should stand out all the time. It's exhausting.

So is taking yourself too seriously.

HAVE a GETAWAY.

Find a dreamy place above the fray—away from dirty clothes and Wi-Fi….a place you can fly to easily…perhaps a favorite coffee shop or a secret park bench.

Better still, build a retreat of your own, a just-for-you place perched on a breezy branch of your imagination.

184

BE CURIOUS.

An inquisitive mind is the only toy you'll ever need. It's the best thing to bring on a date, to the teacher's office, and to a party. In a tough job market, it will be your edge. In boring company, it will be your entertainment.

185

IT'S A LONG AND WINDING ROAD,

and a very small world. We have to take care of one another.

186

DON'T AIR YOUR DIRTY LAUNDRY.

(You knew this would be in here somewhere, right?)

Write in longhand every day.

Whether it's penning a love letter or drafting a thank-you note, write something in cursive with pen and paper. The process puts your brain at a different speed than typing or texting, and experts say it boosts your creativity.

188

BREAK IN YOUR SHOES.

The worst times for a blister are a great date and a bad vacation.

189

HONOR YOUR FEAR.

It may be trying to tell you something.

190

DON'T BE PARANOID.

191

HAVE AN ESCAPE AND RESCUE PLAN.

Even smart, strong women get victimized. If you're on a date or out
on the town and things get scary, use an escape plan you have worked
through in advance with a friend. Crawling out the bathroom window
of the restaurant only works in the movies.

192

DON'T PROMISE A KIDNEY TO SOMEONE YOU MET IN A BAR AFTER 2 A.M.

193

FASHIONABLY LATE IS FOR PARTIES,

not business meetings. *And if it's your party...not so fashionable.*

194

WHEN YOU'RE TALKING TO SOMEONE AT A PARTY, DON'T LOOK AROUND FOR SOMEONE BETTER TO TALK TO.

195

DON'T OVERSTAY YOUR WELCOME.

Certainly this goes for lingering late at someone's home or dorm room, where you should absolutely leave while people are still awake, preferably laughing. It also goes for mere conversations. If you're feeling energized by the company because they are letting you tell all your best material, it may be time to plan your exit. Leave them wanting more.

196

SHOW YOUR JEANS WHO'S BOSS.

197

SHOW YOUR DREAMS WHO'S BOSS.

Sometimes when we dream big, we scare ourselves. We look at what we declared in our biggest, truest moments and decide we were thinking too big. After a string of bad days, we begin to think of our dreams as taskmasters or hard-to-get lovers, and we concoct reasons we don't really want them after all. For shame!

Your dreams are at your beck and call, and don't ever forget it. Their job is to serve you, inspire you, pull you forward, and keep you from eating that third brownie. Make them toe the line.

198

It's okay to OUTGROW YOUR DREAMS.

The dream house of your childhood would not hold your wardrobe today. And the dream job of today may come to feel like a prison sentence tomorrow. What you hope and work for will change as you do, so don't hold too tight to resolutions you may have outgrown. The true longings of your heart: to flourish, to love, to explore, to create… will always be part of you. Grip them loosely, and they will float along beside you, just enough out of reach to keep you interested.

199

TAKE FLYING LESSONS.

Sitting in the cockpit and feeling the plane lift off under your control is a lesson in physics and personal power. You don't have to get your pilot's license or even fly solo, just take a first lesson to see how you like it. A first flight costs less than a facial, and the afterglow lasts much longer.

200

TAKE COUPLES DANCING LESSONS,

so you know how to lead and how to follow.

201

NO MATTER HOW MUCH YOU LOVE AND TRUST A PARTNER, stay in charge of your money, your body, and your state of mind.

202

REINVENT YOURSELF as often as you want. *Just keep the essence that makes you you.*

203

THE TOOTH FAIRY MAY STILL COME. Even though you think you have a lot of things figured out, don't give up on magic. If you lose a tooth late in life, for whatever reason, put it under your pillow.

204

RED STAINS.

Blood and red wine were among the first dyes, so they know how
to stay put. To have a prayer of getting them out, treat them quickly
with a good product.

205

KNOW YOUR BLOOD TYPE.

And if you have type O, negative or positive, donate blood
whenever you can. These types are in highest demand because
they can be given to anyone.

206

KEEP SOME BANDAGES IN THE KITCHEN.

YOU CAN OUTFOX THE SOCK MONSTER.

Yes, the vexing invisible varmint that lives between the washer and dryer is smart. But you are smarter.

Know the enemy. Sock monsters dine exclusively on individual servings—that's one sock of a pair. This leaves you with one lonely sock and an annoying decision to make: whether to throw away the lone survivor or stash it in the single-sock purgatory drawer hoping for its twin to return.

The best protection is the buddy system. Clip or pin your socks into pairs when you put them in the laundry basket. Together, your socks will evade their pesky predator and arrive from the dryer presorted.

Since you are not likely to actually do this, may I suggest buying several pairs of the same socks?

208

COTTON ALWAYS SHRINKS IN THE
WASHER, no matter what the label says. Does this mean don't wash
cotton? No, it just means buy it on the big side, rather than the small side.

209

WOOL SHRINKS WHEN YOU GET IT WET.
And when you dry it, it shrinks some more. Does this mean don't buy
wool? No, it just means don't wash it or get caught in the rain.

210

COMMON SENSE AND SELF-RESTRAINT
SHRINK IN THE PRESENCE OF PASSION.
Does this mean don't be passionate? Absolutely not.

211

GET YOUR LAPTOP OFF YOUR LAP.

Your mother remembers a day when cigarettes were sold as throat therapy, so forgive her if she's a bit nervous about product safety claims. When you hold your computer on your lap and your phone to your ear too long, you may be getting unhealthy doses of electromagnetic radiation. Why take a chance? If only for your mom, put a safe distance, or a headset, between your Wi-Fi devices and your most precious body parts—your brains and your ovaries, for starters.

212

GET YOUR FEET OFF THE FURNITURE.

213

TURN OFF THE LIGHTS WHEN YOU LEAVE THE ROOM. Why is this so difficult?

214

Pick up **THE TAB** sometimes.

Starting out is a unique time in life. Money is tight, and that won't change for a while. But don't be that person who always shows up for the free meal and never reciprocates. Every once in a while, pick up the tab for coffee or snacks.

215

KEEP TABS ON YOUR FAVORITE THINGS.

Be generous. Share your new shoes with your sister. Loan those perfect earrings to your best friend for her job interview. Offer your favorite Spanx to your roommate as she heads out the door for her Match.com date.

But remember to remember who has what. And gently secure its return before too much time goes by.

216

YOU'RE NEVER TOO OLD FOR CRAYONS.

217

FACEBOOK IS NOT FRIENDSHIP.

It's a great way to stay in touch, but if you spend more time online than face to face, you'll miss out on a lot. Hugs, for instance.

218

EVERYTHING'S NEGOTIABLE.

This may not be entirely true, but the people who believe it seem to save a lot of money.

219

YOU WON'T KNOW UNTIL YOU'VE ASKED.

If you want something, ask for it. A raise, a discount, a date, a salad instead of fries—they can be yours for the asking. Things that can make your day or change your life often don't get offered up.

If embarrassment is your only deterrent, know this: most people love to grant requests. How will you know the difference between a person who will say no and one who is waiting to give you what you want? You have to ask.

220

IF YOU'RE FLIRTING WITH EVERYONE, YOU'RE FLIRTING WITH NO ONE.

And you're probably embarrassing yourself.

221

MARRY SMART.

Employ the marriage advice that was once given to men: marry someone who can cook, clean, and raise your children.

222

DON'T MARRY FOR MONEY.

But keep in mind that people who are good with money are usually good at a lot of things.

223

BEWARE OF MARRIAGE ADVICE.

224

YOU CAN TELL A LOT ABOUT A MAN BY THE WAY HE TREATS:

- his mother
- his pet
- the server at Applebee's

225

30-MINUTE MEALS take an average of 53 minutes—plus a trip to the grocery store for the ingredients you forgot.

226

Celebrate **VALENTINE'S DAY,** even when you're <u>**NOT**</u> **iN LOVE.**

St. Valentine would agree. Love's holiday is the perfect time to express your heart to coworkers, friends, and siblings. And, especially, your mom.

THE MESSAGE IS THE MESSAGE THAT IS RECEIVED.

It doesn't matter how clearly or loudly you think you said something, if the person you're talking to didn't get it, you did not communicate. Blaming your audience for not listening will get you nothing but an irritated audience.

So be heard: Speak the right language. Use the right tone. Tell a story. Take responsibility for getting your message across, and you will always have the world's ear.

228

BORING HAPPENS.

Create your own way to enjoy waiting in line.

229

DON'T JOKE IN THE SECURITY LINE AT THE AIRPORT.

230

But try to find humor _everywhere else._

231

IF YOU KNOW HOW TO SELL, YOU'LL ALWAYS HAVE A JOB.

232

DON'T SELL YOURSELF SHORT.

233

CHECK YOUR PAYCHECK.

Make sure you know how much you are being paid and what is being taken out.

234

MANAGING YOURSELF IS THE FIRST MANAGEMENT JOB YOU WILL HAVE.

Do it well, and life will be filled with promotions.

235

MAKE YOUR BOSS LOOK GOOD,
as long as it doesn't make you look bad.

236

LEARN TO DELEGATE.

Then, with the right spouse or personal assistant, you can rule the world.

237

THE BEST WAY TO GLOW IS TO THROW
THE SPOTLIGHT ON SOMEONE ELSE.

238

THE BEST WAY TO HAVE MORE
HAPPINESS IS TO GIVE MORE AWAY.

239

THE BEST WAY TO GET SOMETHING
DONE IS TO DO IT.

240

YOUR BEST IS ALWAYS BEST.

Sure, beating the competition is a rush. And winning or setting records can earn you fleeting attention. But knowing you gave your personal best leaves a lasting satisfaction that no person or team can take back in a rematch.

241

DON'T MAKE EXCUSES.

242

YES MEANS YES.
NO MEANS NO.
Use your words.

243

LEARN JUST ENOUGH ABOUT SPORTS.

And by just enough, I mean enough to master the full array of sports metaphors required to hold your own in a sports bar or a business motivation meeting.

You will need to go the whole nine yards if you want to hit a conversation out of the park and through the goal post without fouling out. Learning the metaphors for key sports is not a sprint, it is a marathon, right down to the wire, the buzzer, and the final whistle. Mistaking a spike for a strike or a punt for a bunt will get you sidelined to the girls B team, and you won't even know the shape of the ball that hit you.

244

CHEATERS RUIN IT FOR EVERYONE.

245

LEAVE IT ALL
ON THE COURT.

If you are going to ROLLER SKATE in the RAiN, at least put some CLOTHES ON.

247

BREATHE DEEPLY.

248

GET SOME SUN.
Vitamin D makes you happy.

249

GET A TETANUS SHOT EVERY 10 YEARS.

250

WHEN FRIENDS TELL YOU TO MAKE YOURSELF AT HOME, remember, it's still their home.

Be such a gracious guest that they really wish you would stay. (But don't.)

251

NATURE NURTURES.

Scientific studies show that a potted plant in the room makes you happier, more productive, and even lowers blood pressure. So learn how to keep a plant alive.

No, artificial plants aren't as good as the real thing.

252

FORGET

bad memories.

253

FORGET

bad hair days.

254

Sometimes,

FORGET

to be afraid.

255

REMEMBER, HOWEVER, TO BE AFRAID OF THE TRULY SCARY THINGS:

of losing your curiosity, of bruising your hope, and of developing bunions, which will severely limit your footwear choices.

256

Remember your mother's birthday.

It's your birthday until you're __HAPPY.__

Why is it that our most special days are often disappointing?

Maybe it's because the anticipation messes with our heads. Or maybe it's because our friends and family are all self-absorbed cheapskates. Or maybe we just run out of time. Twenty-four hours is hardly enough time to celebrate the dazzling miracle of such a birth as yours.

If the clock strikes midnight at the end of your birthday, and you don't feel adequately celebrated, don't pout or be a martyr. Declare an extension. Make dates with all the people who forgot or claimed to have schedule conflicts. They will be touched—or at least caught off guard. And though they may not plan a party, they will probably say, "Happy birthday."

You will soon feel happily satisfied by the attention or happy to let it go for another year.

258

CHOOSE YOUR WORDS CAREFULLY.

259

PROOFREAD, SPELLCHECK, AND
DOUBLE CHECK THE AUTOCORRECT.

260

WHEN YOU DON'T KNOW
WHAT A WORD MEANS,
LOOK IT UP.

261

WHEN YOU DON'T KNOW
HOW TO PRONOUNCE A WORD,
LOOK IT UP.
No, not on your phone in the middle of dinner.

262

NO MATTER HOW MANY POLITICIANS
SAY IT WRONG, the correct way to pronounce nuclear is
"nook-lee-ar" not "noo-kyoo-ler."

263

EVERYONE DESERVES to have her name spelled
and pronounced correctly.

264

DON'T BE THE SMARTEST PERSON IN THE ROOM, EXCEPT IN CLASS.

Evidence shows that people shut down and engage less when they feel they know less than others in a conversation. They also have less fun.

So whether you want people to like you or to help you solve a problem, resist the urge to prove your mental superiority.

265

DON'T BE THE TEACHER'S PET WHEN NO TEACHERS ARE AROUND.

266

SHARE.

267

DON'T OVER-SHARE.

268

LIFE WILL NOT GRADE YOU,
BUT IT WILL TEST YOU.

Coming of age means saying good-bye to feedback for all the work you do. You won't get counted for attendance or get extra credit for neatness. But showing up neatly will be the least that is expected.

You will not know how you're doing compared to others or how many points you need to pass. You will not know your place on the curve, and it won't matter anyway. *Don't worry, you'll get used to it.*

269

EVERYTHING COUNTS.

To get us through the swings and misses of growing up, we sometimes comfort one another with assurances that certain things don't really matter.

The truth is, it all counts—the good and the bad and the barely visible. It counts how we treat people we'll never see again and how we treat people we see every day. It counts how much we try, how much we lie, and how much we rationalize by saying it doesn't count. It all goes into the layered, luminous masterpieces of the people we are. It doesn't make us good or evil or stupid, but it does count.

270

COUNTING ISN'T EVERYTHING.

Don't keep score in friendships, families, or romance. It doesn't work.

271

ENOUGH ALREADY.

You are entering a stage of life that is all about adding things. You'll be adding credentials to your résumé, skills to your repertoire, and friends to your contact list. You'll be testing your capacity, finding just how much you can hold and control, how much you can do and know. Know this first: *you are enough*.

Right here, right now, you *know* enough to make your way in the world. You *have* enough to succeed. You *hold* enough to find happiness. With the family, friends, and faith you possess right now, you can live a life that billions around the world would envy. Most important, you *are* all you need to be. To God, to those who love you, and to the truth within yourself, *you are already enough*.

EPILOGUE

At the time of this publication, my freshly minted college graduate, Taylor Kay, is working in New York City and using all her quarters at the laundry room in her apartment building, which I am told is a very big deal. My younger daughter, Tess, is showing her dreams who's boss at DePaul University in Chicago.

They are smart, kind, creative young women who know more than they let on.

Most important, they know what's important: they know they are loved, and they know that if they ask nicely, I will always do their laundry.

Thank you...

By its nature, motherly advice rarely is original. Credit and profound gratitude go to my own amazing mom, for a lifetime of lessons, and for forgiving all the times it appeared that I was not listening.

Doing the laundry is more fun with company. Thank you to my smart, generous bevy of thought laundresses, proof that if you want something done, you should ask a busy woman: especially Judy Heeter, Julie Nelson Meers, Mary Pepitone, Jody Summers, Tula Thompson, Barbara Unell, Marie Woodbury, and Lindsay Zimmerman. Big thanks to Jill Schram and my E.E. sisters, for loving my girls as your own and for hours of ideas, inspiration, and encouragement. Thank you to my agent, Joanne Brownstein Jarvi, who forgot she was an agent long enough to be a just-in-time editor and muse.

Thanks and kudos to Willoughby Design for classing up my laundry, and to Emily Phillips for countless late-night loads of bubbly ideas and cheerful changes.

This edition will help save the world from more sock monsters and more bad life decisions, thanks to the editing brilliance of Michelle Lecuyer and the talent of Becca Sage, Jillian Rahn, and Liz Kelsch.

Finally, loving thanks to my lifetime laundry partner, Cary Phillips, for being the best kind of dad two girls and a Bichon could have.

272

Always LEAVE ROOM for advice from those who love you.

ABOUT THE AUTHOR

Becky Blades is author and illustrator of *Do Your Laundry or You'll Die Alone*, named a Best Books of 2014 by *Kirkus Reviews*.

Since selling her award-winning public relations firm a decade ago, Blades has created a portfolio life that includes work as a business strategist, creative consultant, civic volunteer, artist, and mentor.

A graduate of the University of Missouri School of Journalism, Blades writes on a range of topics for diverse media.

PHOTO BY 8183 STUDIO

She writes about her daughters and empowering young women at laundryordie.com. Her creativity blog, stARTistry.com, celebrates the art of beginning. At last count, she has started 2,873 projects and finished 132. Among the unfinished are her just-launched daughters, proving her point that it's not what you finish, it's what you START.

Blades lives in Kansas City, Missouri, with her husband of thirty-plus years and her Maytag front-load washing machine.